Wilson Reading System®

Student Reader Eight

Wilson works.

THIRD EDITION

by Barbara A. Wilson

Wilson Language Training Corporation

www.wilsonlanguage.com

Wilson Reading System® Student Reader Eight

Item # SR8AB

ISBN 1-56778-074-1

THIRD EDITION (revised 2004)

The Wilson Reading System is published by:

Wilson Language Training Corporation
175 West Main Street
Millbury, MA 01527
United States of America

(800) 899-8454

www.wilsonlanguage.com

Printed in the U.S.A.

Step 8 Concepts

R-Controlled Syllable

8.1 R-Controlled syllables: **ar**, **er**, **ir**, **or**, **ur** in one-syllable words (**firm**, **turn**, **barn**)

8.2 **ar**, **or** in multisyllabic words (**market**, **cortex**)

8.3 **er**, **ir**, **ur** in multisyllabic words (**skirmish**, **surgery**)

8.4 Exceptions: vowel-rr (**hurry**, **barren**), **para**

8.5 Exceptions: **ar**, **or** in final syllable (**beggar**, **doctor**), **ard**, **ward** (**blizzard**, **onward**)

bark	scar	yarn
start	charge	arm
tar	car	ark
dart	harm	spark
large	farm	dark

or	horn	cord
pork	born	snort
corn	fort	storm
shorts	north	sport
force	thorn	torn

curb	squirt	dirt
herd	stir	fern
burp	sir	her
turn	church	girl
chirp	bird	twirl

burnt	fir	squirm
skirt	swirl	Bert
serve	shirt	birth
curl	first	term
verb	hurt	surf

part	curb	her
bird	porch	jar
burnt	swirl	herd
fork	fern	tart
sir	horn	curl
yard	first	serve
card	girl	spark
turn	chirp	starve
fir	north	burp
squirm	church	birth

lard	harp	carve
harsh	bar	farce
barge	arch	barb
stark	par	starch
marsh	snarl	lark

form	shorn	for
port	dorm	lord
sort	horn	scorch
scorn	scorch	stork
forge	torn	cork

jerk	urn	firm
irk	lurk	spurn
hurl	spur	curt
furl	slurp	whirl
perch	mirth	curve
stern	blur	nerve
urge	clerk	blurt
pert	swerve	thirst
spurt	splurge	shirk
gird	flirt	merge

arch	quirt	storks
farce	torch	hurls
barb	jerk	churn
stern	parch	forge
torn	stark	kern
north	birch	perch
barge	quirk	tern
smirk	chart	berth
scorns	burst	kerf
turf	carve	swerve

quirst	sterb	flurp
pharp	dorp	shern
blerk	swert	smarch
scorf	sparn	borst
flirm	pirsh	spurf

smirt	slerve	tirge
barth	chorp	shorp
sturf	squarm	turl
tharn	swurt	clern
pherd	plirp	glard

1 Can we park the car and go into that fort?

2 The kids had lots of thorns stuck in their pants.

3 Tony's best sport is basketball, but David's best one is tennis.

4 We must drive ten miles north to go to the big baseball game.

5 A storm is predicted, so we must go home soon.

6 My shorts are torn, but Gram can mend them for me.

7 We can sit on the porch and play cards until six.

8 I can start the car and go for a short ride.

9 That yard looks like a park!

10 I would like to have corn and pork pie for lunch.

SUBSTEP 8.1 A   WRS STUDENT READER | EIGHT   9

1 The car had to swerve so it would not hit the girl.

2 Dad burnt the pork on the grill and now we will starve!

3 Emma was first in line for a drink.

4 Did I mention the birth of the puppy?

5 Mr. Lang will serve lemonade on the porch.

6 Did you see that large bird perch on the fence?

7 I selected a pink shirt for Jane's gift.

8 Sandra had long curls that fell to the middle of her back.

9 The pollution will severely hurt our lake.

10 Nancy suggested that the bird was a lark.

1   Enya is so smart that I am positive she will do well this term.

2   This donut is extremely tart!

3   The sunset over the marsh is quite nice.

4   We must help the people so that they do not starve.

5   A baby girl was born, and Bert and Cathy were thrilled.

6   It is impossible to force people to study; they, themselves, must wish to do well.

7   Kirk went golfing and was excited when he got a score of one above par.

8   Mom has the talent to spark people's motivation and desire to do their best.

9   Mark came to the conclusion that he must quickly sort out the mess.

10 Janet is a smart lady and quite a dynamic hostess!

1   It is likely that we could force the opposition into a modification of their stance.

2   In the dark, Marge lost her nerve and ran home.

3   Ginny had to quickly swerve to miss hitting the curb.

4   Barb is consistently stern with her children.

5   Ed and Bert finally got a catch in the lake - five nice, big perch!

6   Jim had a sly smirk on his face, and Peg could tell he was up to something!

7   Take a left, drive six miles north, and then the road will merge with Park St.

8   Curt did quite well with his marks in the first term.

9   Dennis gave his wife a skirt and matching scarf.

10 The girl on probation had to start accepting responsibility for her actions.

Snow Forts

The first large snow storm to hit the city was always the best. The snow drifts in the parking lots were huge and perfect for forts. Joseph and his friends made it a big production. The first ones to get to the parking lot were able to select the best drift. When the forts were complete, a snowball combat was sure to take place.

Phil was the first one at the parking lot after the big storm. He started to dig out one of the tall drifts. Joseph and Fernando finally went down to the lot. They went with Phil's suggestion for the best spot and began digging and packing snow. Tony came, but he was on crutches and couldn't help with the fort. He started to make snowballs and store the ammunition.

When the kids from the next block came over to the lot, they inspected the drifts as well. At last they chose one with a decent position. They started to mark their turf and tackle the job of fort construction. They had to firmly pack down the snow.

Before the forts were complete, the first snowball hit Phil on his left arm. It came from the north and he darted around to see his opponent. The challenge was met. The battle of the snowballs began!

Attack Dog

Donna had to get home quickly. It was getting dark, and she was expected at nine o'clock. She did not wish to upset her mom. She had a distance to go and she had to walk. She had to decide on the fastest way to go.

Donna could turn left at the edge of the park and cut through some yards. That would be the shortest way home. She would have to trespass, but she did not care since she was so late.

Donna went through one yard safely, but as she was passing through the second one, she saw a dog snarl. It intended to chase the girl. The dog barked and attacked. Donna had no place to go for protection. She started to run, but as she got to the curb, the dog jumped on her.

A man gave a whistle and the dog finally ended its aggression. Donna's shirt was torn, but the dog had not bitten her. She was extremely upset.

The man called the dog and got him into his porch. Then he went to Donna to make sure she was O.K. She was shaken but she was fine. The man was very kind. It was regretful that her shirt was torn, but she had been trespassing. She decided that next time she would not cut through other yards. She had been wrong and she learned her lesson the hard way.

The Dorm Flirt

Barb was not very happy. Jan had some nerve! She was such a flirt. Jan tended to stir things up at the dorm. At first, Barb thought she was just being too sensitive, but then she asked her sister, Cathy. Cathy felt the same way; Jan frequently flirted with Ed. She just did it for sport. The girl had to be told to stop. Barb did not intend to let Jan turn the flirting into a romantic relationship.

department	remark	garden
market	carpet	harvest
partner	apartment	garlic
argument	army	harmonica
barnyard	marble	gargle

order	forest	organize
forklift	orbit	hornet
uniform	memorize	morning
porcupine	perform	information
shortstop	transportation	acorn

marvel	pardon	factory
uniform	Doris	tornado
foghorn	victory	Bernard
sparkle	alarm	tardy
organ	margin	unicorn

armpit	farmyard	carnival
carton	forty	torpedo
farthest	Martin	boxcar
yardstick	depart	snorkle
startle	party	sharkskin

cargo	harmony	sharpen
startle	artistic	arthritis
shipyard	bombard	harmonize
harness	tarnish	garment
discarded	darling	starling

parsnip	arctic	arbitrate
armrest	barber	cartridge
charming	embargo	barbell
garble	garland	hardware
larva	carbon	particle

ar

charter	marketplace	compartment
narcotic	charger	starvation
parchment	embark	partake
marksman	pharmacist	radar
partnership	marmalade	scarlet

or

forbid	hormone	formation
organic	cortex	shortcut
deformity	florist	orthodox
conformist	passport	sportsman
morbid	ornament	format

formative	shortwave	corpus
ordinate	deportation	formula
forgery	photography	torso
enforce	platform	transport
record	history	deodorize

horizon	horoscope	torment
escort	border	absorbent
morsel	retort	accessory
corporation	sorcery	originate
formulate	forbid	opportunity

forlorn	partition	reform
hardship	supportive	distort
pharmacy	ornate	partridge
contortion	fortitude	carhop
divorce	participate	garnish

fortress	portion	sarcastic
orthodontist	informative	organization
exportation	incorporate	dormant
varnish	ajar	extort
orthodox	regard	organic

abnormal	enforce	deport
moral	extortion	fortitude
distort	forbidden	ornament
survival	informal	carbon
memory	armadillo	article

forceps	jargon	Arnell
orphan	glory	mortal
misinform	horizontal	sordid
formal	partnership	adoration
ardent	artichoke	vortex

1 Nancy had some fudge at the carnival.

2 My badge has a unicorn on it.

3 The alarm at the mansion went off in the morning.

4 Doris must replace the lost boxcar.

5 A tornado was predicted in Kansas.

6 That factory is gigantic.

7 Martin made the decision to challenge Ken to a swimming race.

8 The farmyard is full of animals.

9 The stars in the sky sparkle.

10 It's so cold, we should go back to the apartment and get a jacket.

1   Barb had to decide who to take for a partner in the game.

2   We have to put this list in alphabetical order.

3   Tony likes the truck with the forklift.

4   Mr. Martin will donate his time to help out at the farm.

5   Carl and Gregory swept the carpet on the porch.

6   Boris will be in the Army until March.

7   The students had an argument during recess.

8   I like all the ferns in the thick forest.

9   The yardstick is in the back closet.

10 We can shop in the department store when we complete our chores.

1   I must organize those messy desks!

2   Ed drove on the back roads to find a shortcut to the marketplace.

3   There is a porcupine in the path of my car.

4   The child was upset when he lost his dark red marble in the vent.

5   We have forty marbles in this box.

6   Don't put the carton of milk on the kitchen shelf.

7   Arnell hopes for a big victory.

8   That club requires uniforms.

9   I hope we can find a shortcut because I am quite late!

10   Kirk will gargle since he just ate lots of garlic.

1 Gregory was born with all the artistic talent in the family.

2 Martha made a nice remark about the attractive garden.

3 My partner sold the surplus harvest.

4 Irving imported the lumber and turpentine.

5 Martin squirted the garments with liquid.

6 Bernard flirted with his latest darling.

7 My mom forbids me to go to Tom's apartment alone.

8 I think it will be difficult to transport the brass bed.

9 Ed discarded the useless, old harmonica.

10 The detective was in charge of the narcotic drug bust.

1   Bert must memorize the formula in order to pass the test.

2   I ate garlic, so I must gargle before I go on my date.

3   Even after taxes, that large corporation made a big profit.

4   The planes will fly over the target and bombard it.

5   Carla must organize these terms for the next quiz.

6   The girls in the band harmonize so well!

7   Cindy must find an apartment in the city, but she is finding them so expensive!

8   Our company will try to form a partnership with that successful firm.

9   The pharmacist helped me select the best remedy for my cold.

10 This belt will make a good accessory for my scarlet dress.

1 Bart will help formulate the supportive organization.

2 Let's get the ornaments and garland from the attic.

3 Carmen is an artistic florist.

4 I do not like artichokes in my salad.

5 Marcus had strong survival skills.

6 Did the car accident result in Carl's memory loss?

7 Mrs. Porter will attend the formal garden party.

8 I must find a carbon copy of the plans.

9 We will celebrate the glory of victory!

10 Did the harmonica startle the children?

Ed and His Harmonica

Ed discarded his old harmonica and went to the store to get a new one. He wanted to practice the instrument so that he could sharpen his skills. He had to refine his talent so that he could harmonize with success.

Ed had a second floor apartment. The people on the first floor did not mind when Ed made his music. They were in the band as well! Soon Ed and the band would perform on stage. It would be a thrill.

Partners' Dispute

Marcus went to the lumber yard, and his partner, Tommy, went to the hardware store. In this way they could get to the job site by ten a.m. It was so hot! They were planning to complete the job by one o'clock and then quit for the day.

Marcus had difficulty at the lumber yard. They did not have the trim in stock. When he went to the job site, he told Tommy and Tommy went wild. They got into an argument but it did not last. Marcus wanted to go to a lumber yard in the city and Tommy wanted to quit for the day.

At last a decision was made when Tommy tossed a penny. They would quit for the day. Marcus was unhappy so he packed his things and left.

Martin's Morning Off

Martin had so much to do on his one morning off! He had to be at the office by twelve o'clock so he had three hours to complete all his tasks. He had to go to the orthodontist, make a trip to the department store and pick up a prescription at the pharmacy. He felt it was impossible but he was willing to try. With a little time organization, it could be done.

Martin was glad when he quickly got called to see the orthodontist. The visit did not take long at all! As he drove to the department store, a dog suddenly ran into the street. Martin had to swerve to miss the dog, and when he did this, his Ford truck hit the curb. The dog went safely across the street.

Finally Martin got to the department store. He was able to find his items quickly and there was a short check-out line. He became confident about the completion of his tasks. Then he went to his truck. The tire was flat! He had not expected transportation problems.

By the time he fixed the tire, he had no time left to stop at the pharmacy. He was lucky to get to the office at eleven forty-nine. He was not late for his job, but he would have to get the prescription on his way home.

The Garden Party

Mrs. Rosicott, a stylish lady, was planning a garden party at her home in Concord. She had a charming yard, and with her artistic hand, it would be perfect! She had a remarkable talent with plants. She would not have to call a florist - her yard was already filled with floral decorations.

Mrs. Rosicott made a garland of scarlet roses to hang on the trellis. She ordered a large tent from a local rental agency. She would pick bunches of fresh flowers to make it elegant.

Many people had responded to the invitation to the garden party. It would be a smashing success! Mrs. Rosicott ordered the food and made the final plans. Then she sat back in anticipation of the fun.

burlap	shiver	interest
survive	plaster	surgery
intercom	sherbet	Irving
disturb	Germany	blister
bakery	turnip	circus
enter	sturdy	thirsty
turpentine	return	consider
Irwin	cucumber	perhaps
concern	grocery	cursive
refrigerate	advertisement	thirty

government	remember	November
October	Bermuda	pester
pepper	sunburn	birthmark
corner	zipper	supper
temper	whisper	chapter
termite	muffler	member
border	carpenter	purple
summer	winter	butter
batter	number	slipper
dinner	sister	operate

thunder	canter	splinter
monster	corner	river
remember	turtle	curler
silver	ladder	letter
whisker	operation	ruler

over	pitcher	super
paper	clever	northern
lobster	pattern	dirty
surprise	better	pepper
under	September	person

spider	desert	lantern
never	panther	perfect
energy	understand	partner
perfume	matter	hammer
curtsy	circle	Vermont

mineral	rubber	disturb
offer	litter	butler
circulate	fertilizer	hamper
locker	gardener	officer
forever	ginger	thermostat

merchant	Virgo	mercy
circumvent	surmise	murky
persist	surpass	furnish
temperament	confirmation	exterminate
intervene	infirm	incinerate

regurgitate	insurgent	sulphur
pulverize	absurd	verbatim
gangster	skirmish	insurgent
perspire	irking	convert
murder	perplex	persistent

filter	elder	somber
referendum	allergy	interstate
veranda	mercy	tavern
conserve	alert	revert
intern	commerce	turban

yonder	ember	shimmer
cancer	sputter	hermit
expert	rudder	mutter
diner	banter	banner
lattery	submerge	properly

gallery	administer	bursitis
persist	meter	pottery
burden	gurgle	confirm
murmur	prosper	differ
suffer	bitter	poker
fodder	fiber	foster
turbulent	platter	misunderstand
imperfect	converge	permanent
percolate	tolerate	ponder
admiral	hurdle	birthrate

girdle	turnstile	surly
archery	modern	chipper
taper	filter	sober
invert	saber	tinder
circumstance	scamper	surplus

observe	proper	supersonic
messenger	copper	insert
stutter	excursion	archives
urchin	turnpike	perjury
skirmish	miser	caper

prefer	superb	quiver
cider	clover	plunder
consider	kindergarten	vermin
burden	amber	further
urban	furtive	femur
nursery	slender	timber
suffer	master	serpent
adverb	verdict	permit
gender	sermon	general
crater	concern	clatter

1 Jennifer will perform up on that platform at five o'clock.

2 The spark came from under the car.

3 Phil went to the grocery store to get cucumbers and olives.

4 Put your dirty shirts and shorts in the hamper.

5 I understand this subtraction problem.

6 The surprise party for Alexander was so much fun.

7 Mom likes her gift of perfume and Dad likes his lantern.

8 Set the lobster on the table!

9 Jerome picked the number five car to win the race.

10 The girl did a fine curtsy to the king.

1   The pup was quite clever.

2   Did you ever try lobster with butter?

3   My sister had to sit in the corner for a punishment.

4   Is that person in the white dress from Vermont?

5   Mark never got the instructions for the quiz.

6   All of this excitement is from the thunder.

7   Norma is from a northern city, possibly Toronto.

8   The carpenter had a solution to fix the broken swing.

9   Robert thinks it is fun to plunge into the cold river.

10 Termites have made the bridge unsafe.

1   It is important to save energy.

2   The fender on his car is bent from the accident.

3   Cut the paper into a six-inch circle.

4   Buffalo can be so cold in the wintertime.

5   Can you name the states that border Vermont?

6   In the spring the turtle crossed the path and slid into the pond.

7   Where is the location of Bermuda on this map?

8   Kirk had a sunburn on his back.

9   Do you remember the location of the entrance?

10 The athlete whispered advice to her pal on the bench.

1 The misunderstanding makes me sad.

2 The judge plans to give her verdict at twelve o'clock.

3 That last hurdle will be the most difficult.

4 I must insist that you perform your dance for the club.

5 Perhaps a hornet bit her, and she is allergic to it.

6 Try not to interfere with Gregory's plans.

7 Marcus lost his membership card for the club.

8 Hopefully, the chess master will permit the competition.

9 The pottery on the porch is nice, but rather expensive.

10 I hope that we can survive this turbulent storm.

1 We must reduce the risk of cancer since it takes so many lives each year.

2 Joseph was covered with blisters after he finished his tasks in the yard.

3 The gangster was convicted for a big robbery.

4 Irma had to go to Germany for surgery on her hip.

5 The letter is in cursive form and too hard to decipher.

6 We can refurbish this home, but first we must carefully consider the cost.

7 Perhaps Cliff will serve the plum sherbet.

8 There are termites in our home and we must exterminate them.

9 The runner did persist even though he felt cosiderable pain.

10 The advertisement cost to the merchants is absurd!

1   There was a big disturbance at the bakery shop this morning.

2   The cops had to intervene in the argument between two men.

3   The smell of sulfur is quite disgusting.

4   Betty will start her internship in just thirty days.

5   Mom felt the bursitis in her arm when she had to lift the grocery bag.

6   The salesman was persistent, but the company still had little interest in his product.

7   We did not like the turnips with ginger!

8   Jerome went to the hardware store to get turpentine.

9   The trees are being harvested at an alarming rate by the lumber company.

10 Dad will ponder the question before he makes his decision.

1 The considerable birthrate will surpass thirty percent.

2 Peter's lung cancer made him so sick.

3 We will not tolerate Jennifer's bad temper.

4 If you order gingersnaps in the bakery department, I will return with sherbet.

5 Did Irwin participate in the skirmish?

6 The farmer harvested surplus turnip.

7 Government must reaffirm its interest to conserve forest and marsh land.

8 Conserve the plaster so that we can cover every wall.

9 Insert the porcupine in the sturdy burlap bag.

10 She must survive surgery for a heart murmur.

1   The merchant expected confirmation of the advertisement.

2   The story ended when the serpent returned the girl to her home.

3   Bertha has the temperament to intervene during turbulent times.

4   Bert is thirsty, so he will percolate a fresh pot of hot coffee.

5   With a shiver, Omar turned the thermostat to circulate the heat.

6   Germany will consider how to enter the marketplace.

7   If bursitis enters the arm, it can persist.

8   Carl's concern reflected his mercy.

9   It is necessary to convert to this cursive method.

10   Can Curt refurbish the old furnishings?

Equipment Problem

Wisconsin was hit with a turbulent storm. Snow is common in Wisconsin, but this storm hit quick and hard. Parts of the state were covered with twelve inches of snow. It left a huge mess all along the northern border.

Many merchants had to close shop. The temperature was below zero, and the blustery wind made it difficult to see directly ahead. Drivers could not travel and many were stuck shivering in their cars. Electricity was lost in many locations. Some people did not get it back for days.

The clean-up in the state took several days and cost quite a bit. Although it was such a bad storm, all residents did survive.

The Baker

Irving ran a bakery in Ohio. He was still single at the age of forty-five. He did settle down even though he did not have a family. After work, he did not ramble around the town. He went to his apartment and had a quick dinner. Irving was not able to read, so he would turn on the television to occupy his time.

Irving was the sort of man that had no cares on his mind. He did his job and had little to concern himself. He was happy with his life for the most part.

Then one day, Irving met a lady, Martha, in the grocery store. She had lost her husband in a car crash and was left alone with five children. She was a fine and interesting lady. Irving and Martha had lots of fun. Irving met her children and took them places on the weekend.

After awhile, Irving had to decide what to do. He had to consider many things. It was a big decision, but it did not seem difficult. One nice summer day, Martha became Irving's wife. It was quite an adjustment for Irving, but he was a very happy man.

Save the Forest!

Jenny became interested in the forest land in her home state, Minnesota. The trees were being harvested for lumber at an alarming rate! This disturbed her as well as many other concerned citizens.

Jenny felt that regulations had to be enforced before it was too late. The state did have many trees to conserve. A considerable number could be harvested, yet too much was being taken from the national forest lands.

Jenny persisted until she formulated a recovery program. She wanted the government to stop selling the trees in the national parks. There would still be plenty of lumber without disturbing some sections of the state. Jenny's plan was supported by several congressmen. She felt that her concern could help motivate further action to save the trees.

hurry	correct	sorry
Harry	territory	interrupt
barrel	worry	porridge
terrible	horrible	marry
hurricane	carrot	errand

Larry	ferry	Gerry
carry	cherry	terrific
surrender	berry	correction
merry	barrel	interruption
Terry	parrot	Barry

terry	scurry	herringbone
sherry	barracks	horrid
cirrus	correlate	barren
burro	barricade	corral
irritate	correspond	currency

tarragon	ferret	corrode
derrick	flurry	tarry
interrogation	current	narrate
irrigate	curriculum	erratic
irritation	herring	corruption

paragraph	parasite	paraphrase
paragon	paramedic	parable
paradox	parasitic	parataxis
paradise	parallel	parasol
paravane	parasang	parapet

ar-vowel

aroma	aromatic	arena
arid	aristocrat	arithmetic
Arabic	marigold	arise
arose	baritone	tariff
arum	sarong	maritime

1 Barry had to hurry to get the telephone.

2 The kids did not surrender their fort.

3 The gentleman in the garden shop is a terrific person.

4 Gerry and David went on an errand to the department store.

5 I think the parrot in the cage just said "Hello."

6 We should all worry about the bad pollution in this city.

7 Larry corrected all the arithmetic problems.

8 The television interrupts my concentration.

9 Can we hide in that huge barrel?

10 I suggested that mom skip the carrots and just serve the chicken.

1   My dog likes to protect his territory.

2   I will convince Terry to try the porridge.

3   Cindy thinks that lotion smells horrible.

4   Larry was sorry that he missed the circus.

5   Harry has a terrible cold, but still he must complete the report.

6   I hope we can catch the ferry to Nantucket.

7   I will not be able to carry this barrel when it is full.

8   Jan must hurry home to make the cherry jello for the mold.

9   Cherry is the berry for my porridge.

10   Martha felt terrible and was sorry that she interrupted her dad.

1   That fabric tends to irritate my skin so I do not use that garment.

2   My best grade this semester was in the current events class.

3   We must try the herring appetizer on the menu.

4   The gangsters set up a fort with a barricade to stop any intrusion.

5   The class elected Gerry to narrate the story.

6   The army did not intend to surrender quite yet.

7   Sherry plans to marry Dick next October.

8   Let's not make the corrections on the report until it is completely finished.

9   Pete was sorry to interrupt the boss, but he had to get a copy made quickly.

10   The hurricane left horrible destruction along its entire path.

1   Larry Mason led the interrogation to uncover corruption in the company.

2   The high school staff requests suggestions for the new curriculum.

3   The acid that spilled will quickly corrode your car.

4   Gerry tends to make erratic decisions for his sales territory.

5   The dance corresponded to the tempo of the merriment.

6   An interrogation was held to stop the corruption.

7   Bake the carrots with ginger and curry spice.

8   The cirrus clouds in this territory may bring us a flurry.

9   Use the derrick to lift barrels over the barricade.

10 Watch that ferret scurry for the herringbone.

1   Plans to irrigate this state will carry water to barren places.

2   Larry did not hide his irritation with the lazy burro.

3   The herring will have to hurry in this swift current!

4   Harry is irritated by his terrible grade in algebra.

5   The pilot of the ferry was irresponsible with her navigation.

6   You must find the correct terry cloth.

7   Must James run the errand in this horrible hurricane?

8   The prisoners will be interrogated after they surrender.

9   Gerry is the merry old man in the circus.

10 We must get a serrated blade while on errands.

para

1   I wish I had a parasol to block the sun.

2   Jim has to study quite a bit in order to become a paramedic.

3   Harry had a bad fall last winter that might paralyze him for life.

4   The joggers' path runs parallel to Barren St. along the river.

5   It will be paradise to vacation in Florida in December.

6   When I complete this last paragraph, I will be finished with the report.

7   It is important to protect your dog from parasites.

8   When you do this term paper, you must not paraphrase.

9   I like the parable about the fisherman.

10   Jane will enter the parallel bar event in the gymnastic contest.

ar-vowel

1 Larry wished to get an invitation to dinner after he smelled the aroma from the kitchen.

2 I think it must be quite difficult to graduate from the Maritime Academy.

3 Jake arose and went to the department store with Kerry.

4 During vacation we can go to the arena to skate.

5 Cindy helped Gerry with his arithmetic problems, then he asked her for a date.

6 The cactus grows well in the arid desert.

7 This credit card will help satisfy my aristocratic taste.

8 We must arise at six in the morning in order to make it on time.

9 Cara made a fantastic shot in the basketball game.

10 The digits we use are Arabic numbers.

Algebra Class

Larry sat with frustration in algebra class. He felt terrible because he did not understand, yet he did not want to ask irrelevant questions. The circumstance always made him upset.

Larry did worry about his grade in algebra. He was not irresponsible, but he could not pass in his homework when he did not understand it. He did not like to interrupt the teacher to ask for assistance. At last he surrendered and went up to the teacher. She made several corrections and helped him do the problem. She could tell Larry was trying and she was more than willing to help.

Sidetracked

Harry and Gerry were freshmen at Surry Community College. They were twins. Harry was generally quiet, but Gerry could be a bit wild. At times, Harry went along with Gerry and ended up in a predicament that made him sorry.

One Saturday afternoon there was a prediction of a possible hurricane. There were no candles or lanterns at the twins' house, so Harry and Gerry were sent on an errand to get a lantern at the store. They had to hurry back to the house.

At the store, Gerry saw two friends - Tom and Pete. They were on their way to Tom's house to "hang out" during the storm. Gerry felt the temptation to go along. Gerry had to first convince Harry. They made the decision to tarry just a bit at Tom's house before they went home.

The twins' mom began to worry when it suddenly became darker. She did not think that the boys were irresponsible. She felt they must have been in a car accident.

Gerry and Harry forgot about their errand. They were in the middle of a dart match. The lights flickered. It reminded them of their responsibility, and they quickly left to scurry home. When they saw their mom they had to confess. They felt terrible that they had made her worry so much.

para, ar

Cara's College Plans

Cara had the desire to go to Clern University. She filled out the registration form. She took the S.A.T. test and another entrance exam. It was quite difficult! She had to read several parables and paraphrase them. She also had to write five paragraphs defending a position on a current topic. Lastly, she had to complete a math section. This did not have basic arithmetic - it had complex algebra, geometry and calculus.

Cara gave the test her total concentration. It was well worth the effort. In late March she got the letter of notification in the mail. She was accepted as a student at Clern!

beggar	doctor	dollar
inspector	tractor	harbor
flavor	major	razor
motor	cellar	minor
favor	conductor	vinegar

governor	similar	janitor
alligator	elevator	regular
corridor	collar	popular
instructor	actor	armor
solar	inventor	calendar

nectar	Oscar	sponsor
splendor	stellar	contractor
tartar	investor	sculptor
humor	labor	clamor
odor	rumor	tutor

vapor	candor	vigor
lunar	glamor	stupor
valor	tumor	manor
error	vigor	mentor
tenor	projector	ambassador

terror	savor	factor
caterpillar	polar	globular
protector	peddlar	rigor
mortar	stellar	fervor
ardor	cedar	vulgar

protractor	disfavor	ancestor
donor	monitor	granular
navigator	particular	pastor
burglar	grammar	censor
collector	pillar	vulgar

wizard	orchard	mustard
custard	backward	blizzard
northward	sideward	standard
forward	homeward	westward
hazard	lizard	upward

haggard	onward	scabbard
tankard	drunkard	windward
gizzard	afterward	inward
buzzard	laggard	Richard
Willard	innards	mallard

ar | *or*

1   We must replace our puppy's lost dog collar.

2   Take the elevator rather than the steps.

3   I think that twenty dollars for these tickets is much too expensive.

4   At the end of the long corridor, take a left.

5   Brenda hopes her company has solar energy.

6   The pelican likes to fish in the harbor.

7   Give the conductor your ticket.

8   Did Richard see that huge alligator?

9   If you find out the location of the game, it will be a big favor to me.

10   The regular television program is not on this channel.

1 The janitor in our school is a very kind man.

2 I think the smell of vinegar is disgusting!

3 Sammy hopes to become an actor and Martha wishes to be an actress.

4 I recommend that you get advice from your doctor.

5 Wendy is popular with the kids in her class.

6 First I must check the calendar to be sure I can make it on that date.

7 The bad odor of sulfur made me sick.

8 Did the doctor operate on his tumor?

9 Terry's dance instructor is Mrs. Martinez.

10 My doctor suggested that I rest but I want to play basketball.

1 The actor had mustard on his chin.

2 My grandmother made custard when I was sick.

3 Cara is a forward on the basketball club.

4 It was difficult for the people to travel westward in covered wagons.

5 A blizzard is expected to hit the Northwest states in the morning.

6 Carmen likes her pet lizard and Boris likes his hampster.

7 That unsafe bridge is a hazard.

8 Can we pick apples in the orchard?

9 We will go homeward after the last competition.

10 The wizard could not convince us with his tricks.

1 If you just ignore his vulgar statements, he will stop.

2 Betty Morten should get an Oscar for her terrific performance.

3 Trevor is so artistic; he is a sculptor and an illustrator.

4 The contractor will get a new tractor for big jobs.

5 Let's have dinner at the place on the harbor.

6 I hope I win the fifty-dollar first prize in the class contest.

7 The new home uses a combination of solar and gas energy.

8 I was lucky to get Mr. Merlin for a gym instructor.

9 The company must hire an inspector for the new product line.

10 The collector was glad to find the armor in the castle for sale.

1 Ed is muscular from the construction job.

2 The supervisor had to check the progress in the cellar construction.

3 Sandy did not do well in grammar, but she got an A in geometry.

4 The club must vote in a successor for the role of president.

5 It would be nice to find an investor with lots of cash to spend.

6 In order to communicate, we should have a translator here!

7 The ambassador from France is visiting Florida.

8 We will ask several contractors to bid for the job.

9 Major Hernandez is the navigator for the polar ice cap mission.

10 We expect the cold to be a particular problem.

ard | *ward*

1 Carla was inwardly upset about the five game suspension.

2 Oscar went forward despite his depression.

3 Is Mitchell on the windward side of the dock?

4 Cindy felt haggard after all the confusion.

5 I suggest spicy mustard on that ham sandwich.

6 The army will march onward until the destination is reached.

7 The standard evaluation form must be submitted to the boss.

8 There are many lizards in the tropics.

9 The lack of restrictions could prove to be a hazard.

10 The persistent buzzards are above the sick cattle.

ar | *or*

Return to Splendor

The large harbor was disgraceful. The condition of it had become intolerable over many years. A bill was passed in Congress to clean it up. It was a popular project with little opposition.

There were several bids for the harbor cleanup job. It would be done in five phases. A supervisor was selected for Phase I. An inspector would then decide whether or not it was done to satisfaction before the Phase II contract was signed.

Hopefully, the harbor could be returned to its splendor of the past.

The Solo Investor

Oscar was a mad inventor. He did not pay any attention to the calendar. He did not attract investors and he was not popular with his family. et, Oscar had vision. Long ago, he made the decision to work on a solar activator. He went to a sunny, isolated place in Arizona. He spent most of his days in solitude with his activating equipment. He did not think of it as his hobby - it was his destiny. He did not even feel as if it was a gamble. He just had to do it. Oscar did not wish to get rich, though he could have used a few dollars. Oscar merely had to perfect his life's vision and make an effective solar activator to be used for energy.

A Blizzard Crash

Doctor Spencer was homeward bound in the midst of a terrible winter blizzard. He intended to progress onward even though the roads were a hazard to overcome.

As Doctor Spencer turned the corner on Tannard Street, he saw a car across the road. He had to stop quickly. Then he rushed out of his car to see what had happened.

A man indicated that two cars had collided, and one went off the low bridge into a frozen marsh. The doctor acted fast. He was able to pull the driver from the car and administer the necessary care. An ambulance came, and it became evident that the man would survive the crash. Afterward, Doctor Spencer was glad he had been there to help.

Post Test Step 8

conductor	organize	intercom
terrible	thirsty	marble
mustard	flavor	hurricane
cucumber	partner	squirt
cherry	serve	blister

B

arbitrate	exterminate	successor
orthodox	sulphur	vulgar
forgery	surrender	westward
circumstance	interrogate	muscular
ancestor	paraphrase	deformity

Post Test Step 8

Nonsense Words

sharving	surdy	blustard
reporm	temperize	transvisor
sportion	plerry	prentar
phertent	burrid	arint
exfirm	paravide	placery

1   Underline or scoop syllables.

2   Circle r-controlled vowels in each word.

3   Mark r-controlled exceptions with a breve (˘) if the vowel is short.

4   Mark /ər/ above any **or** and **ar** that say /ər/.